FABRIC

Poems

Lucinda Roy

FABRIC: Poems

Cover design: Lucinda Roy and Larry E. Jackson

Cover painting: Lucinda Roy, "Suffering the Sea-Change: The Carver of Masks," used by permission of the artist.

Author photo: Larry E. Jackson

ISBN 978-0-9985278-1-9
LCCN 2017931087

Willow Books Editor's Choice Series

Willow Books, a Division of Aquarius Press
www.WillowLit.net

Printed in the United States of America

To survivors of violence around the world

and to L, J, R & A, with love

BOOKS by Lucinda Roy

FICTION
The Hotel Alleluia
Lady Moses

POETRY
The Humming Birds
Wailing the Dead to Sleep

MEMOIR
No Right to Remain Silent: What We've Learned from the Tragedy at Virginia Tech

Acknowledgments

With thanks to the editors of the following publications where these poems originally appeared:

"Animal Vegetable" in *American Poetry Review;* "Disarmed" and "Diamonds in the Rough" in *Blackbird;* "Mussels" in *Callaloo;* "Severing Ties" in *The Cimarron Review;* "At the Aberdeen West African Fistula Center, Freetown" in *Crab Orchard Review;* "Stone Kite" in *Hawai'i Pacific Review;* "The Ceremony of the Dead," "Madonna in the Bush" and "Texting: A Ballad" in *Measure;* "Orogeny" in *North American Review;* "Primary Circles" and "A Mind Full of Winter" in *Poet Lore;* "Camera Obscura," "Cordon Sanitaire," "Detention & Multiplication," "Fabric," "Our Waiter Wasn't Wounded" and "Stealth" in *Prairie Schooner;* "Machetes: Several" in *Rattle;* "A Majority of One" and "American Angelus: An Immigrant's Ode" in *River Styx;* "Custodians of the Bush," "Narrative Arcs in Hindsight" and "On the Syllabus Today: Blue Skies" in *Superstition Review;* "Childhood Garden: Battersea, South London" typographical rendition in "Unleashed," an exhibition, Moss Arts Center, Virginia Tech; "End Words: A Sestina" featured in *No Right to Remain Silent: What We've Learned from the Tragedy at Virginia Tech* (Random House/Three Rivers Press); "Ga Wree-Wre: The Judgment Mask" in *Arts Meets Literature: An Undying Love Affair,* a special publication by the Library of Virginia and the Virginia Museum of Fine Arts.

Contents

III.   American Angelus: An Immigrant's Ode

END NOTES

PART I: War Zones

O, I have tae'en
Too little care of this!

—*King Lear*, Act III, scene iv

A Majority of One

I am the only passenger on the top deck of the double-decker at a time of day
when London's buses can be sanctuaries—assuming skinheads in their steel-
toed bovver boots don't mount the narrow winding staircase at the back of
the bus and discover me here on the top deck in the Rosa-Parks front seat —
coloured, female, alone. The 137 bus rocks through London, its high center
of gravity a liability. As a child, I'd been a passenger on a bus when it slammed
into a motorcyclist. At the moment of impact, the bus shuddered and snorted
like a bull. The man spun out from smoking tires to land far away, as if he'd
been swept out by an asphalt tide, his pale, bald, unscathed head as puzzling
to my child eyes as his stillness—his face slammed into the pavement, his
khaki-colored, Inspector-Clouseau mackintosh puddling around him like an
epilogue. But that was then and this was now the seventies. Black is looking
in the mirror; Black is raking its hair with a pick. You're grown, ensconced on
the top deck, sitting at the front in the Rosa-Parks seat. Below you, through
the grimy windows as you ride southwards across the River Thames, the city
lurches from privilege to want. You're reading English with the pedigreed at
King's College, London; you're a veteran of Topshop's clearance sales; you
wet your hair to make your biracial Afro stand to attention. Risky to let your
hair be your hair—a disavowal of the white majority, a graphic dialect. But
your hair belongs to you so you do it anyway. You glance down at the dirty
cream-colored panel beneath the grimy window where an Englishman has
used his pen as a sword, gouging seven wounds into the skin of the bus: *All
niggers should be gassed at birth.*

You know the author means it; you know the author means you.
You know you are a disquieting metaphor, a fusion of un-likes.
You know geography can be a tyrant, prejudice a war monger.
You know the cage isn't where the Black bird sings, it's how she dies.
You know you will leave this overcrowded island with its pessimistic sky.
You know it may not make a difference—the sky is ubiquitous and
                                                    unreliable.
You know you love your white widowed mother as much as you love your
                                                    dead black father.
You know Shakespeare and Dunbar, Brontë and Hughes.
You know that the double-barreled *g* in *Nigger* is a shotgun.

You know this, too: *You are here on the top deck—un-gassed and well read.*
You understand that masks have a tendency to suffocate their wearers.
You dismount, careful not to trip as you descend the winding stair.
You step off the platform in your red high heels.
You are not a child—after an assault you've learned not to sob or scream.
You walk down the High Road toward home, wearing your small brown
face like a native.

Cordon Sanitaire

In the tropical rainforests, Ebola's found
in the fruit bats of the Pteropodidae family.
Flying mammals. Bush meat. When it made its debut
in the seventies, the zoonotic virus decimated
a village near the Ebola River in the country
known then as Zaire. Scientists named it after
the nearby river, fusing water to disease,
life to death—only their maps were wrong.
Ebola, "the Black River," wasn't the nearest river
after all, but by then it was too late.
Maybe in the future local people will adaptively
mutate the Ebola River, linking it with the source
of contagion in much the same way as the mob
in Monrovia mistook health workers for carriers.
(Only a fool trusts faceless, body-bagged aliens
who incinerate your noble dead *without marking
their exit with touch*—an irreverence so unconscionable
it turns tears to blood.) When you walk through Freetown
it's like walking on the skin of a drum.
The city's shuddering paucity vibrates around you,
a Gregorian secular chant of *Need, Need, Need.*
Clinics and hospitals are empty of equipment and packed
with people waiting patiently to be saved. Children share beds
in the ICU—a ward so Dickensian it's unnerving to step
outside and find cars and electricity. Last time I was there,
hemorrhagic fever was waiting in the wings, which explains
why hope wasn't yet amputated from circumstance.
Armageddon leases this part of the globe
from the British and the French. Every day a disaster-
thriller—minus the stars, financing, and spectators.
(If a child dies and no one honors his journey
does he really die?) The beautiful burned boy
in the dupled bed was photogenic
enough to be a star. Yesterday, when news
of the Black Death flickered across CNN's ticker-tape,
cordon sanitaire sounded humane. Today I watch

games of hunger, refuse to permit a boy's indigestible
smile to play havoc with my Greek yogurt and goji berries.
More bats will be eaten, more dead will lie in state
to be touched by villagers who knew them.
A mother will kiss the tears of her boy
because he's dying and the cord can't be cut.
A black river runs through us, a microscopic worm on a string.

After Therapy, a Villanelle

the heart's a cracked window, a thief's way in
four horse-powered chambers, four mouths that speak
damage is peripheral, feminine

strangers can enter, bend like light unseen
sex turned into frantic hide and seek
the heart's a cracked window, a thief's way in

inside the chamber pumping is routine
some forms of suffering deserve the term *unique*
damage is peripheral, feminine

the thing you yearn for most is to be clean
cleanliness is godliness and you're a freak
the heart's a cracked window, a thief's way in

suck the death star, tastes like nicotine
dancing's what you did once, cheek to cheek
damage is peripheral, feminine

all is up and all is in between
every word translated by his shrill physique
the heart's a cracked window, a thief's way in
damage is extensive, feminine

Making Progress: A Poem for Two Voices

We are making progress, the president tells us, *but it is slow.*

A small delegation of women, we are at the State House
in Freetown after the conclusion of war. We do not go
anywhere without a security contingent. It's not paranoia;
it's caution. Like women everywhere, we travel in a convoy

We are making progress but it is slow.

of empathy. We're here to study infant
and maternal health. When the boys show
their absent limbs as they beg for Leones I don't look
in their combustible eyes lest I tumble in.

We are making progress but it is slow.

When I lived here, British tourists still came to the Bintumani
Hotel. All men are islands when abroad. An archipelago
of expats proved that neo-colonial gatherings were still alive
and well and Graham Greenish. I had haggis at the Bintumani once.

We are making progress but it is slow.

A mere girl, I was not afraid to walk down Big Waterloo
Street alone. The nation was relatively un-wounded. Although
doctors were still rare, of course, they hadn't all escaped.
We've been helicoptered upcountry, toured bush hospitals and clinics.

We are making progress but it is slow.

In the city, refugee-residents build houses from shipping cartons.
There's no profit to be made for incarceration so the country doesn't throw
its young black men into prison. It embraces a mandatory rhetoric
of Truth and Reconciliation, an obligatory absolution.

We are making progress but it is slow.

It's an inspiring example of extraordinary forgiveness
they say—how an amputee mother foregoes
vengeance and lives peaceably next door to the machete-man
who placed her armless baby in her armless arms

We are making progress but it is slow.

because she must. Like Greene I wrote about my times here,
made a little money. Black gold mined from a wound-well. My novel
oratorio with its ensemble cast of characters. The curtains in the president's
office are a blood-red velvet. *Theatre*, they whisper. *Dust.*

We are making progress but it is slow.

Cooled air slugs it out with the heat; guards look straight ahead.
In rows of chairs lined up in front of the president's desk we're a rainbow
coalition. Diamonds were the country's ruination—ubiquitous, alluvial,
hopelessly easy to mine. Progress is more rice, more used prosthetics,

We are making progress but it is slow.

universal education for children in primary school.
DeBeers was concerned when the overflow
of bodies rubbed the pretty off diamonds. It took time
to polish the crap off the stones and pry them out of the black

We are making progress but it is slow.

market, but with so much at stake they found a way to do it.
(Administering CPR to a nation bitten by war is slow.
You have to position your mouth just so, press down hard
near the heart, before you can rid it of cytotoxins.)

We are making progress but it is slow.

We are a small delegation charged with conveying our findings
to 10 Downing Street and back to the U.S. We've arrived glowing
with good will. We wish there were more than two
pediatricians in the country but we are realists.

We are making progress but it is slow.

We visited a ward full of malnourished toddlers
getting plump on *Plumpy'Nut.* An embryo's
development is the lot of girls in the developing world. Most are under-
developed themselves. The problem in a nutshell.

We are making progress but it is slow.

On the streets of Freetown, children (many lovely
enough to grace the cover of Vogue,
some with war wounds so savage they make you stutter)
sell us knick-knacks—lighters, gum, peanuts.

We are making progress but it is slow.

I taught here in the good old days when you could travel
from Freetown all the way to Kabala and know
you'd never have to pass a single amputee
camp. We return to maternal and infant health—a hard nut

We are making progress but it is slow.

to crack when one in eight women die
of complications during pregnancy. I dip my toe
in amniotic fluid, pull it back. I carry a pen
even though I know words can be a careful washing of feet,

We are making progress but it is slow.

a pedicure. Sentiment plays pimp to the poor
however large its eyes may be. In Freetown, we don't overthrow
anything. It's beyond our powers to do so. Instead,
we bestow our insufficient gifts.

We are making progress, the president tells us, *but it is slow.*
We thank him for having us. The tremolo
in the State House is the status quo.
We women come. We women go.

1 X 4: A WAR REQUIEM

I: Diamonds in the rough

When Sierra Leone is at war, boy soldiers are prized.
Conditioned to be as boastful as Hummers, they are proud
of the way their mirrored sunglasses wink in the musky light.
Words like angst and remorse are as strange to them as calculus.

These children know their catechism: *koppoh, titi, dedebodi**
and *RUF*. Like children they find comfort in their favorite colors—
the marine blue on the headscarf worn by "Massacre"
(the boy from Masingbe whose murder count impresses
even the captain), the pineapple yellow of T-shirts stolen
from the mission after Massacre diced up the garrulous priest
while he was still preaching.

Turned on by the screams of women, by movies
projected onto sheets tacked to the pitted walls of classrooms,
they are loyal when it suits them, treacherous when it doesn't.

In the Eastern Province they sing,
High we exalt thee, realm of the free
Great is the love we have for thee **
as they riddle a village with bullets.
In the Northern Province they crack
jokes as they slosh through blood.
Stallone sings them lullabies.

They are boys cubed—testosterone made nuclear.
They have learned from us the sadism of want.

At night, by the fire's kindly light, their bare child-eyes—
lovely, complicit—sparkle like diamonds.

---

*   *koppoh, titi, dedebodi*: Krio words for money, girl, corpse.
**   The first lines of Sierra Leone's national anthem.

II: The Ceremony of the Dead, Sierra Leone

On the rim of hell, though peace can come undone,
the wretched of the earth—the desperate ones
formerly tattooed by terror—have begun
to expect to keep their hands. They no longer run
like rabbits when a car backfires; the gods
they pray to limp towards a UN epilogue.
Children construct an anguished catalog
of wishes: rice, prosthetic limbs, divining rods.

This is the land of fevered pendulums
where people cling to civility's gnawed rope.
At night it's Halloween: severed hands tend
graves; politicians chant, "Fee-Fie-Foe-Fum,"
brandishing tin cups and guns while Hope
makes small talk, and Justice stumbles to make amends.

III: Detention & Multiplication

The soldiers stormed the school in the afternoon.
Everyone had left. Everyone except the boy
in detention, and his mathematics teacher,
Mr. Mathora—"a fine name for a math
teacher," students used to say. A soldier-boy
in a blue headtie found them hiding on
the high school's pineapple farm inside
the storage shed the Peace Corps built before
he left for good. The boy in the blue headtie
yelled to the others who came running,
as if the soldiers were students who'd been let
out of class early that day, as if this were
a celebration. The rebels (men and boys)
pulled up the pineapples that suddenly
looked to the detained boy like severed heads
being yanked from their graves. They cut up
the fruit along with Mr. Mathora.
The detained boy stopped at that moment—stopped
growing, stopped feeling, stopped knowing who he was.
The detained boy didn't hesitate when
the rebel captain commanded him to spit
on his teacher's remains. At the time it seemed
appropriate—his teacher had failed
to prepare him for what lay ahead.

On the road, the detained boy grows to love
2 things: first, the way his G3 feels
as he lashes the worn strap over his shoulder;
and second, the way his head floats to the tops
of palm trees when he's high. It's then that he
gives himself permission to be anyone
he wants—a daredevil, a paramount chief,
a giver of mercy, a butcher, a friend,
a priest, a teacher even…. The other boys
call his rifle *Girl3* because he snuggles
up with it at night. They say he's so eager

to kill a few more villagers he never
leaves his girl alone. He doesn't tell them
the real reason he keeps it with him.
Doesn't say that, without it, he'd wet himself
with fear. He's learned to watch his mouth because
he wants to keep the rest of his teeth.
The rifle calms him. If he could slip it
in his mouth and suckle on it he would,
but he's scared of that too because he's 9
and not a baby, and there's a lot goes into
figuring out what comes next after a move like that.
Fact is, Mr. Mathora shouldn't have detained him.
That was the trigger. Each night, when he's sober
enough to remember the pineapple farm,
the boy forgives himself for spitting on
Mr. Mathora's fractions, forgives
Mr. Mathora for not teaching him
the things that matter. The detained boy recites
the only tidy words he can remember,
the ones he likes to use as chaperons:
1 x 1 is 1; 1 x 2 is 2....
Mathematics is a prayer he wants to
remember always—something sweet, something
logical, something easy to digest.

IV: Disarmed

He is still those boys at night when his dreams
are laced with genocide. When day breaks
and the armless beggars wander down Big Waterloo Street
he vaguely recalls something distant and obscene.

Two years of school taught him the potency
of humiliation. Some days back he saw his real teacher, the Captain,
speaking with a white man in a suit outside the bank.
He wanted to run over, fall at his feet,
beg the Big Man to take him back into the fold.

Weary of petty crime he's ripe for another thrill ride
on the blade of a machete. He says nothing out loud
to anyone: the Captain taught him the value of patience.
He knows one day the call will come again and, when it does,
he'll be the first to sign up. He's not afraid
of death—his or other people's. He knows what they see:
a homeless Temne,* a *bobo*,** a dog.

Something bubbles inside his head. He lies
awake at night by the fetid open sewers
and listens to militias of rats on food raids.

Disarmed and dangerous, the child waits for democracy
to spring a leak.

* A tribe in West Africa.
** Krio word for a small boy.

Our Waiter Wasn't Wounded

Our waiter is a small, modest-looking man
who bears a story so large it drives the heels of his calloused feet
into the ground: the story is the sledgehammer; he is the stake.

There's a lot at stake in Sierra Leone. Men live 38 years; women 42.
In his forties, our waiter is an old man. He's glad my husband and I
aren't White—*you'll be able to hear my story*, he says.

His story is told without bitterness. At our invitation he sits with us.
We're the only patrons eating breakfast on the terrace at 4:30
in the afternoon; we're all messed up when it comes to time zones.

We're all messed up. This is what I understand after his story.
Now the war is over I'm here to find my students.
Our waiter looks out over the bay. *It was very bad*, he says.

Evil arrived in hordes waving guns and machetes above its head,
streaming down the streets of Freetown. It had to kill
everything that moved. It pounded like a piston, throbbed like a wound.

Our waiter wasn't wounded. When they broke down the door
to hack off his hands or blow off his face he had the presence of mind
to beg for his life—a small thing to them. He offered them a large thing:

all his small money. They took the cash and didn't maim
or murder him after all. Maybe there was honor among thieves
or maybe they'd grown bored with maiming and executions.

Death defecated here, the breeze whispers. On the balcony's white
balustrade so-called minister birds strut in their clergy-ed self-importance.
Behind us, Kimbima Hotel sways and trembles in the heat.

Ex-pats, sweating in the heat, are coming back to Sierra Leone at last.
America has built an embassy-fortress on a hill, far from the stench
of Freetown. A new normal is strapped to the old like a prosthetic.

Prosthetics are hard to come by after the war.
Beggars, even if they have them, don't wear them.
Visitors are more generous when stumps are visual aids.

No beggars near Kimbima. There's security—some of it armed.
Our waiter can't forget the rebels' sadistic question: *Long sleeves
or short sleeves?* An orgy of amputation: *Chop, chop, chop!*

Chop is the Krio word for food. I don't use it. I say *food* instead
as if I never lived there, as if I never learned anything. *Things are better now,*
our waiter says. Overhead, a Russian helicopter does not crash and burn.

The rusty Russian helicopter we flew in from Lunghi airport crashes
and burns a month after we leave, killing all those onboard.
But today it flies above us as languidly as a mosquito.

During the war, flies worked on the mound of corpses piled in front
of the post office. Without emergency responders to remove them
it took a long time for mutts, vultures and rats to have their fill.

We are full, I tell the waiter. *Cassava leaf stew is my favorite.*
It's cool out here on the spacious terrace by the pool
that's always as empty as the shirt sleeves of beggars.

Our waiter's sleeves are frayed. From this same balcony a few days later
we see a school of dolphins. They leap from the water in half-halos,
make us believe in superfluity again, take our breath away.

So much taken away from this land where breathing is labor.
Our waiter stands up, shakes our hands, looking to all the world
like a modest man with a story small enough to grasp.

Lesson Number 1

God's a wishbone old fools pull, so Mattie
doesn't pray. It's Saturday and Master
Quincy entered earlier. His hard stench
rises from the blanket, sour as old milk.
Forgetting where he forced her hand she licks
a ragged fingernail to turn the page—
gags, curses. She stole her mistress' book.
She cannot read the words but fondling them's
enough. Words are secrets, words are stars—
peepholes in a Carolina sky.

With her tongue she feels the tooth he broke
4 weeks ago. He spun around in fury
when she let slip she knew the president's
2 names. *Why'd you make me do that, Mattie?*
Now you ruined that pretty l'il smile.
Best thing that ever happened to her.
Now Quincey's mortally afraid of her
dog-mouth. Makes her keep it closed. Doesn't grab
her neck and guide her down to suck unnaturals
anymore. Doesn't even crave a kiss.
Quincey likes to lay his egg-head on the
platter of her flat black belly when he's
done. Soon as he leaves she shoves a corncob
up her sausage where he's pumped her full of
Quincey meat, makes damn sure she'll never hatch
a thing of his. She knows that if her belly
grows she'll plead with Vesty to make the poison
tea Sela and Tomala drank. Sela's
didn't work. Tomala was lucky—birthed
a perfect dead-born, see-through as muslin.

Quincey's at the Big House with his wife
and little girls—4 living, 2 dead. Sometimes
when she's baking Mattie hears his fever-
killed playing with their dolls. The girls return

from shadows whole, flesh included. Blonde,
blue-eyed, pockmarked, they order their rag dolls
to do their bidding. If ghosts could die again
she'd murder them just to mute their chatter.
Instead, to take her mind off ghoul-speak,
Mattie counts to thousands as she bakes.
Men's numbers are the key to everything—
5-and-7 niggers tethered to the farm;
5-0-4 strides from her cabin to the woods;
15 miles to the river; 6 steps to cross
her cabin, 10 steps to mark its length;
16 hands for Billy Ben's vicious horse;
20 lashes from BB's whip if he's feeling
like he needs some exercise; 40 days
since she snatched the little praying book
from where Mistress Carsy flung it. (Flung it!
A *book! Jesus!* Cast aside as if it was
a corncob or an apple core! She yearns
to grind the witch's face into the pages
of the praying book until the woman's
pointy little nose is flour.)

Today Mattie cleaned the Big Clock. Its pendulum
swung back and forth like a lynching rope,
keeping decent time for the Bridderwells
and filching it from everyone else. Mattie
knows the number for hope is the same as the one
for despair. It's **1**. Effie was the **1**
she loved, the **1** whose wet bead she'd rub to flame,
the **1** who dared to run first. The **1**
the dogs caught.

       Mattie spits on her finger,
traces the secret number on the virgin
end of her blanket—a small pole with a hook
at the top for snagging things. It quiets her.

She grabs the blanket's soiled end, writes
her spirit-number over it to mortify
the stain: **1**. A small spell, impregnated
with desire, pressing itself into her
like Effie used to do, making her moan
like a girl.

AFRICAN MASKS: A Dance Sequence

African, Dan culture (Liberia, Côte d'Ivoire)
Ga Wree-Wre Mask, 19th-20th century
wood, metal, fiber, cowrie shells, glass beads, brass, bone, hand-woven cloth
47"H x 16"W x 22"D
119.38 cm x 40.64 cm x 55.88 cm
Note: Raffia skirt is not original
Virginia Museum of Fine Arts, Richmond. Adolph D. and Wilkins C. Williams Fund
Photo: Katherine Wetzel   © Virginia Museum of Fine Arts

Ga Wree-Wre: The Judgment Mask

I recognize you, *Ga Wree-Wre*. Once
you spoke the language of leopards. In the filtered
light of the museum, protected from
termites and heat, you'll last indefinitely—
though now no spirit-dreams beget you. Far
from the forest of secrets you have no
interpreter, no symbiont, no Poro
Society votary. You are a mouth
that cannot move.
                        As a child, I remember
seeing your brothers in masks my father
carved. For centuries, in Accompong—
the birthplace of my Maroon(ed) father—
the tradition of the carver was passed
from father to son. Five thousand miles away
from the people of Dan, relocated
Africans like him remembered you.

I am your daughter, once removed, but I
would never have been granted the honor
of carving you, *Ga Wree-Wre*, or becoming
your porter. Even so, my lineage is yours:
the mane of cowrie shells framing your head,
your beard of small bells, your crusader's cape,
your cast-down eyes, your intransigent beauty.
The monoxylous carver didn't make you his—
what fool would try to own a spirit-god?—
he made you for them, and it was to them,
the village, that you spoke in your animal-
tongue behind the wooden door of your face.
Mask without a man, African-Diasporan,
antique mannequin of wood and shells
and bone resting on your yellow raffia skirt
(as stained as a kola-nut-eater's teeth)

looking for all the world like someone capable
of sleep, you are *Ga Wree-Wre*
in hibernation.

                    I lived where you once lived.
In my spine is something fossilized.
Among the Poro patriarchs and the
matriarchs of the Bundu, I dispensed
with Time—as if it were a cage I'd lived in
formerly before I found a key.

Outside at night in Africa were stars
as intimate as rain; outside at day
were sudden citrus sunrises, orange
enough to make my wide eyes sting. If you
are wise, *Ga Wree-Wre*, you will keep your secrets
underneath your magic cape and skirt. Don't tell
us that you see inside the dark—we'll picture
flashlights and fluorescent bulbs, we'll never see
your path through time, a leap from here to more
intently *there*.

Ga Wree-Wre, they say you are no dancer.
(What judge would risk such spontaneity?)
Instead, you perform the spoken word—
a duet between persona and interpreter.
Yet what are words if not a dance from pronoun
to imperative, from a dialect
of mercy to an idiom of something
else—from *he* to *she*—from you, *Ga Wree-Wre*,
to me?

Love: A War Triangle

African, Kuba Culture (Zaire)
Mukenga Mask, 19th – 20th century
Raffia, cloth, leopard skin, wood, cowrie shells, glass beads, string
19½"H x 17"W x 22"D
49.53 cm x 43.18 cm x 55.88 cm
Virginia Museum of Fine Arts, Richmond. Arthur and Margaret Glasgow Fund.
Photo: Katherine Wetzel   © Virginia Museum of Fine Arts

I: Mukenga Mask—King of the Kuba*

He took away the sunshine when they banished him for loving
his sister, Mweel. The Democratic Republic of the Congo
was his original home. In Richmond's museum he is well behaved.
He says nothing. Like the Trinity, sometimes he is king; sometimes elder;
sometimes son. His god-name is Woot. The men who played him
weren't gods until they donned this bloodred-skyblue-sunyellow-
mudbrown-bonewhite mask (such color, such audacity!)
with its curved probiscus arcing from its skull-pinnacle,
covered in white-lipped cowries and multi-colored beads.
In a place where each thing is precious and nothing is easily stitched
together, each bead, each shell is toil. He who wears a fountain
of cowries on his trunk and a five-tiered cowrie necklace must be a god.
Or a charlatan. Or a man. History has turned the king's homeland
into a French absurdist play. "Gaga," says the gun.
Blessed with more than a hundred different political parties—
almost as many as the beads on a king's head—the Congo River Basin
writhes like an eel while the West fishes for minnows.
When the Belgians ruled there were fewer Christians and more masques.
In those days, the mask was a rival to be mocked or maimed or kidnapped.
But that was a long time ago—masks were still the dance-stars of the tribe
and Belgium was as much a convert to rape and mutilation
as Kony's Lord's Resistance Army. Today, in the Museum of Fine Arts
the King of the Kuba is mask-still. In his Princess Leia cowrie-shell
earmuffs, his surreal leather nose-ridge stitched with white beads,
geometric flaps on either side of his head, he rats on
Picasso the magician, who pulled Africa out of the hat of Spain.
The King of Kuba doesn't care. His name is not Mobutu or Kabila
or Kony. He isn't a bloodthirsty bastard; he is driven by memory,
which is why—like history—he is a refugee from his own ravaged land.
The museum is his camp, its high walls his tent. Among strangers
he is safe and unrecognized. Organic and manufactured,
a collage of color and shape and need, he is the Mukenga mask,
the god who ran off with Mweel, his sister, taking the sun and the crops
with him, leaving his people to starve in the dark until Mweel pled for
mercy. He is a thing made into phenomenon. He stares at us from behind

_____

*   The three masks are part of the same dance ritual.

his fearful white eyes. He is no *thing*. Unchecked, he sews famine and darkness. His people know him. His real name is Woot.

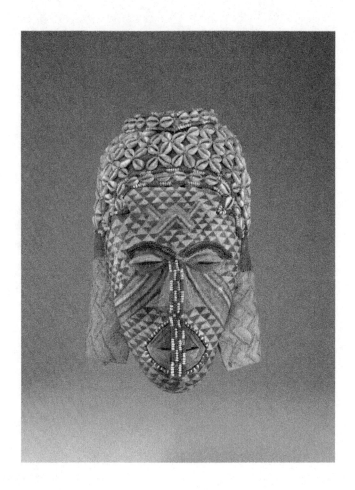

African, Kuba culture, Democratic Republic of the Congo
Ngady amwaash Mask, 19th-20th century
wood, paint, cloth, cowrie shells, glass beads, string
12½"H x 8"W x 9½"D
31.75 cm x 20.32 cm x 24.13 cm
Virginia Museum of Fine Arts, Richmond. Arthur and Margaret Glasgow Fund.
Photo: Katherine Wetzel   © Virginia Museum of Fine Arts

II: Ngady amwaash Mask: His Sister, Mweel*

The stripes of paint beneath Mweel's heavy-lidded
eyes are meant to represent her tears.
Her brothers loved her not unwisely (for she
was worthy of their love) but too well.
Mweel's scarified tears are always speaking.
Tears as insistent as these can make a girl
go mad. Long ago, Queen Ngokady
introduced this mask to celebrate
the role of women. But girls must never dance
inside the mask of Mweel, warrior of mercy.
Men are the only ones allowed to wear her.
Mweel's cheeks, forehead, and chin mutate to math:
her face asserts the artist's fascination
with geometry—the heady relationship
of one shape to another. Snow-white and sea-
blue triangles adorn her—miniature
mountains in a sea of snow, white peaks
over blue shadow. Her elaborate
hair is fashioned into cowrie-stars; her eyebrows
beads of blue glass. She is wood; she is flesh
transfigured by wood; she is vice versa. She
is the sister, Mweel—the one who knows
the word for love is tears. Dangling
from the space between her blue, determined
bead-brows a triple thread of beads. On
her forehead, extending upwards from the slash
of tears on her cheeks, the peak of a
dust-colored pyramid, or an artist's gesture
to expressionism, or a stylized rendition
of a frown. Her mouth is pursed—
ready, perhaps, for a stolen kiss
or an escape of the Last Breath.
She tells us nothing we can know
and everything we can feel.
Her expression is a secret she plans to keep.

---

*   Mweel, the sister of Woot and mother of his child, is said to have persuaded
Woot to show mercy to his people.

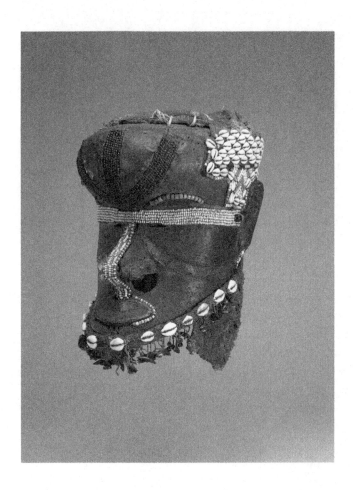

African, Kuba Culture (Zaire)
Bwoom Mask, 19th - 20th century
wood, copper, cloth, glass beads, cowrie shells, seeds, fiber, string, traces of paint
19¼"H x 10½"W x 15½"D
48.9 x 26.7 x 39.4 cm
Virginia Museum of Fine Arts, Richmond. Adolph D. and Wilkins C. Williams Fund

Photo: Katherine Wetzel   © Virginia Museum of Fine Arts

III: Bwoom, Mask of the Brother*

The brother-competitor for Mweel's affections, Bwoom completes
the love triangle. In his role as Everyman, he is a conjugal threat—
the brother with more to prove and more to gain. Therefore,
he must throw himself into the synchronal dance like a man
who knows what it means to lose everything.
His lips and cheekbones are inlaid copper; red, white, and blue beads
follow the contours of his strong nose. Instead of hair,
cowries, cloth, and beaded chevrons adorn the plateau of his head.
His ears are unadorned and startlingly male, as if he is determined
to emerge from formalism to claim his own individuality.
The least stylized of these three masks that trace the royal Kuba line,
Bwoom is the most ordinary among the dancers—the one closest to flesh
and farthest away from emblem. Slashed across his invisible eyes
is a narrow band of white beads. But Bwoom the seer is not blind
when the dance lifts him up and propels him towards divination.
At those times, he is not intimidated by Woot's multi-colored proboscis;
all he sees are Mweel's tear-scars, his sister's agonizing tenderness.
At those times, Bwoom's frantic feet become his eyes, wild with desire.
On his bulbaceous forehead Bwoom's trident of blue beads
catches the light; his pugilistic chin is lined with a single row of cowries.
He is wood and cloth, seeds, beads, and string. He is anything
the artist could find to work with. The brother is darker
than the other two, more pugnacious. Like his brother and sister,
Bwoom's wearer must not be known during the dance.
He is a joined entity, a way of being eternally alive in the bush,
a gesture of significance spawned by history and failure, desire and the
dance. If a drum were to personify itself it would be Bwoom.
Woot and Mweel evangelize but Bwoom apostatizes;
he tells us that all allegiances can be broken by muscle and yearning.
Bwoom wants Mweel. He leaps towards his re-engendered
neighbor-brother-sister.** She in her gorgeous mirror-mask sees him.
For a brief time, God-who-always-is (his brother) and Love-not-to-be (his
sister) will join Bwoom in his dance.

---

*   Bwoom represents Woot's brother and is a rival for Mweel, their sister.
**   In most African mask rituals, female characters are traditionally played by males.

Machetes: Several

Men: several. Night: one.
The year—1979. At 23 I was as wily as
cow dung. Took me several minutes to realize
I'd been invaded. Half-asleep, I saw male forms
moving around my room—men with a purpose.
I took umbrage—chased them with a broom,
slashing at the one who fled through the window,
his ashy leg the last thing I saw before he disappeared
into the bush. When his calloused foot got caught
on the window ledge I batted at it with my witch's broom.
God, I was an idiot. But half a dozen armed robbers
had been *in my room*. Having flown all the way
to Freetown on a British Caledonian jet
I took umbrage. The picked-for-prettiness-and-language-skills
"air hostesses" had worn Scottish tartan tailored into fetching,
figure-hugging outfits that yelled *demure* but whispered
bosoms. In those days they came running
when you pressed the button overhead,
even when you were sitting in coach.
Apart from the nuns there was no one
to whom I could report the armed robbery.
They tut-tutted and told me to hire a night
watchman—though you couldn't trust Africans,
they added, so be careful. I'd stopped reminding them
my father was black—water off a duck's
back. Around the nuns' whitewashed convent
was a stark white wall as welcoming as a chastity belt.
You needed rappelling equipment or a bishop's ring
to scale it, which was why the nuns were left
alone. That and Father Stefano, who had a rifle.
(And Jesus, of course, who didn't.)

Machetes: several. Me: one.
On the corrugated tin roof that night—deluge.

In the decades since, rain and robbery
are as intertwined in my head as women
and service used to be.

They stole the silver ring my mother
gave me. Worth almost nothing
it was the thing I missed the most. They tried
to take my savings book, too, which was why I chased
them and made them drop it. Banks in Sierra Leone
wanted proof of deposit, and my savings book
was all the proof I had that I'd been squirreling away
every penny so I could fly home after a year to see
my mother. My little red savings book was as precious
to me as Mao's book would be to a communist.
I missed my mother, my best friend,
the way a nun would miss the Eucharist.
I was pitch-black lonely.
I'd been allowed to bring one suitcase
to last me two years. I'd stuffed it with "T's":
t-shirts, toiletries, terror and tampons.
I brought my boom box and Stevie Wonder
to make the bush feel more like the South
of London, where I used to sit in my hungry bedroom
like a fool and dream of saving something
very grateful, something very large.

At the Aberdeen West African Fistula Center, Freetown

The young woman with the fingerprint-whorl braids
sits on the bed under the window.
She does not speak much but she is happy.
Now men in her village will know her again.
Infants will hold her hand.

The girl with the fingerprint-whorl braids
woven by a woman's dexterous fingers sits on the bed
under the window, barefoot but dressed in her best clothes.
She does not know what to say to these women visitors
who come and go speaking of the unnatural flow of urine
and feces, nodding when the doctor describes the operation.
But the girl is happy not to be a leper. She will not stink anymore.
Men in her village will call her name. Children will call her "Mother."

The child with the fingerprint-whorl braids
woven by a mother's weary, dexterous fingers (which moved
across her daughter's pretty head with more tenderness
than other fingers, making her daughter believe she can be happy)
this child sits on a bed and speaks shyly to the female
visitors who talk of *obstetric fistula** as if it weren't a
clawing fist but instead a thing domestic—these wrist-watched,
unencumbered women who move on with the doctor
have seen what they came to see: you—a mended mother,
sewn up and ready for the next round of birthing,
going back to your village whole, your stench no longer taunting you,
the foul hole closed, the leak plugged, the plumbing as good as new.
As a child-mother of stillborns, all you have left to focus on now
is this repaired flesh, sutured and pink, healthy and healing and muscular.

The glorious absence of effluence, the eagerness to tell the boys no.

---

*   Obstetric fistula (a hole between the birth canal and other organs) is common in
many parts of Africa where women give birth without access to medical care. The resulting
discharge often leads to sufferers being ostracized by their communities.

Camera Obscura

She dreams of crushing *Viagra*
into dust and hurling it into oceans.
If whales became sudden Casanovas
beating their lusty tails and breeching up a frenzy
it won't bother her. Whales are not men.
Out of the corner of her eye, she sees herself
rocking and rolling with the man who rode her to hell.
She shouldn't have to see that. Better to look
through kinder apertures—the church, or the psychiatrist.
Sometimes, regally, with the conviction of a feminist,
she rides the light as if it were a stallion—
sits astride it, breathless, subordinating it to her will.
Like David Copperfield (the illusionist not the child
of the illusionist) she makes the laws of physics
as compliant as an old celery stalk.
She can do this because she's a woman over fifty.

But then, alas, the summer ends and pinholes start to prick.
The sour tongue revives its familiar, dull invasion,
digging out the fillings in her molars, loosening the bridge
the orthodontist (a kind man but a man nevertheless)
inserted with tenderness to rectify her smile. By now
she has been realigned and resurrected just about
as much as she can stand. She's bored to death.
So today, twenty-eight years after the attack,
a team of male detectives will try to figure out why
she did it when they find her naked on the chessboard vinyl
floor of her master bathroom, her eyes suffused with joy.

Balanced on a ledge as thin as a razorblade just above
the bald detective's head she'll witness their clumsy
game of clues. She won't give a damn when they don't get it right
because, in this new place (where time is light-made-manifest),
she can already see that vile stump of a word with pinhole clarity—
                    Rape!.... Rape!.... Rape!
dancing itself to death on the folds of her own magnificent wings.

PART II: Domestic Science

"And withal they learn to be idle, wandering about from house to house; and not only idle, but tattlers also and busybodies, speaking things which they ought not. I will therefore that the younger women marry, bear children, guide the house, give none occasion to the adversary to speak reproachfully."
—Timothy 5:13-14, *The Bible* (KJV)

MI NA WATASAISTON: A N☐ DE MUV.
I am a waterside stone: I'm immoveable.
—Krio proverb, Sierra Leone

Mussels

Having been mistaken once again for the other black couple in town
we take our seats at the table, order with the rest.
When the subject of race comes up during appetizers (for me
steamed mussels in white wine with tarragon; for you nothing—
as usual, you're saving yourself for dessert) I am chewing.
I think our tablemate is referring to the electoral race at first
before I understand my error. This one is tough—its nacreous, butterfly
shell swings shut on its hinges, small black wings locked like a mouth.
The others at the table are expectant as though we're about to share a
secret. The mussel lodges between my teeth. A toothpick would be
handy. I should have ordered soup.
Sometimes white women I don't know tell me they find him—
my husband—attractive. Sometimes I smile. Sometimes I don't.
Prying things open takes effort and sometimes I'm too tired to do it.
Sometimes I think about the ball and chain dragging along behind
the dangerous feminine. But tonight I eat steamed mussels swimming
in wine and tarragon. We're all filter feeders of some kind or another.
It's the only way to survive.

When you were younger, single, you were mistaken
for the black man the police were looking for—who, apparently,
could have been your twin. You were hauled in for questioning
but then, like the fish in the nursery rhyme, they let you go again.
How easy it would have been for them to keep you.
I duel with another mussel, try to be civilized. My black
husband was permitted to mature out in the open. My black
father, on the other hand, died at fifty-one. The English doctor
broke the news to my mother saying she was better off
without him—my mother being a young attractive white woman
in 1961. I reach for another mussel. It clings to its shell like something livid.
I jab it with a fork and twist hard. It will not detach itself.
Our tablemate is saying she likes Obama. Finds him attractive,
articulate. But why, she asks us, is he so...so...
Obama, son of Abraham, cuff-linked to a house as white as Snow White,
when will the wistful weltering world
stop expecting you to croon it back to sleep?

Animal Vegetable

I grow underground like a carrot
in the library quiet of the earth where nothing breaks.
A voice as blunt as a shovel is ready to disinter me
to haul me up into the incendiary light.

But it's dark and warm down here in Wormville
without the fury of imagery.
Nothing stalks anyone; no one I'm obliged
to listen to calls my name.

Some of us break in two during the unearthing,
but the unbeautiful ones (the stubby ones,
with the bumps and the blemishes like me)
have a better shot at making it.

The voice calls again:
Carrots and sticks! Sticky carrots!
Unplugged like a tooth I am learning to live
beside craters—
soil-mouthed animal
vegetable scream.

No More Clothes

The skin is the most didactic of all our organs.
It teaches us what feeling feels like—
how to avoid pain, how to appreciate chemistry.

Skin's a bandage, an infinitely responsive casing,
the one natural shield we have
between ourselves and the predatory world.

How secure the porcupine must be knowing touch
can't flay him. Thick fur would be an easier
garment, I think. Or scales, like the ones salmon wear

or, better still, the scales sported by dragons.
Feathers, on the other hand, frighten me. I suspect they'd be
even more reactive than skin, flap-flapping

in the wind, sensing miniscule changes in currents.
Wings are what our arms would be
if they were musical instruments.

Like hummingbirds and falcons, refueling tankers conjoin
mid-flight with others of their species. Like love,
the grim ecstasy of war makes aerial coupling worth the risk.

But my vagina is nothing if not a demilitarized zone,
and this is just to say I went off on a tangent
earlier, and though I'm not talking about grimness,

I *am* talking about ecstasy, about plums surreptitiously
eaten. I was afraid to fly inside my skin machine
with you as co-pilot until that unilateral move of yours

flayed me in a good way. Skin so delicate and dark,
nakedness so unassuming, parts so male and escargot.
And there you have it in your hands. A poem? Genitalia?

Mine? Yours? Does it matter? O my skin
toys with yours touchingly. Nothing is long ago.
On the floor beside the bed a funeral pyre

of underwear. Silly garments, deflated silhouettes,
pitiful laundry—shadows of who we were before
we leaped from the puritanical clothesline

and left these ghouls behind. Clothes-less,
we are more *We* than we know what to do with.
40 square feet of skin for us to play inside. Sensational.

Cloacal Night in its muscular, orifice-laden shroud turns us
into stars. Did you know dark-colored feathers are more
robust? Did you know they're less likely to fray?

Sing cutaneously of feathers, of pores
of sweat, of things crepuscular....
All is dark and kin tonight. Our skin sings Alleluia.

Renovating Eden

Without a key or formal invitation, you enter homes
for tips. HGTV is as reliable as banks used to be
before they screwed themselves with sub-prime betting.
There's divinity in a French-polished fireplace,
in a heavy-as-death granite countertop with a lurid shine.
Faucets are angels, arched handles their wings.
It's about grace—about exquisite angles forcing you
to your knees in the privacy of your own home.
After the makeovers there are legions of complementary fabrics,
pillows with karate-chopped V's. Demolish, rebuild, tear down
all the walls! Everything depends on joists and I-beams
the fragile space between *what is* and *what could have been*
if only a little support had been forthcoming. Your skull is a room
in need of a paint job. You have stenciled the wallpaper
with words for *Here* and now it's as yellow as the sun.
Your home is an open concept grafted
onto a closed one. Ease is what you crave—the resolve
of bark on wood. Tear down the fourth wall, let them all in.
Don't say "cheese" and suck on your quartz pacifier,
Wife of McHouse. The sky is a storyteller
riding a light carousel. Get brain-naked. Go outside.
Listen (if you dare) to the cenobitic choir of trees.

Stone Kite

Hope springs eternal is not the kindest adage in the world
it is the most compassionately savage.
Poets are right: stones are sermons. Still,
as a woman descended from slaves, it was my duty

to believe in flight. My stone kite bucked in the wind
rose for a millisecond before it dragged me down.
Life unravels countless spools of grief it preached as we plowed
a grave together, headstrong woman and headstone kite

slave and free. A good student, I held onto the rope
that tethered the stone that didn't fly—
held on for dear life. Now I lie
breathless, without hope.

Above me the stone sways back and forth—an elephant mourning her
dead. It howls and moans with old teeth. Bleached as bone,
the stone—as primitive and obdurate
as the word implies—prepares to sing.

And then the annunciation—stone turned flesh,
a canticle to buried lies
as the rooted albino monolith (attempting kindness)
sings of its terrible yearning to fly.

Edible Sonnets

I: Sea Vegetables

Neither plants nor animals these algal
biomonitors are the canaries
in our sea mines. Their ancient, lacy strands
sing of salt and warn us to lay off the arsenic.
Phosphorescent Nori in its tailored sheets
as dapper as Cary Grant in *Arsenic*
and Old Lace takes up the theme of bloody
history, of something rotting down below.

But it's hard to give a damn about heavy metal
residues when taste seduces you.
Nutrient-dense seaweed snacks, laced
with wasabi, Dulse's iodine-laden
hullaballo, and Nori-wrapped sushi
haiku-ing its kelpish aria to the sea…
                              and to me…and to me…and to me.

II: Pasta: An Exegesis

Eggs, flour, and salt should never taste
this good. Pasta's about coupling—with virgin
olive oil & strumpet-ty garlic, with pancetta
licentiously fatty, with fresh pesto
brazenly green. Pasta's about texture—
strings plucking flavor from their celestial
accompaniment. Shape is to pasta
what God is to the pope—the alpha

& the omega. And when the sauce
is devilishly fine, Eucharist and pasta
become one. Flagellate yourself with fettucine.
Prostrate yourself before a bolognese.
God is found in a pocket, an elbow, a strand.
What weaves the banal into the divine is now and ever shall be the hand.

III: Salt

When briny diamonds beckon, I am no
Odysseus. Before arterial hyper-tension
was current, salt served as currency.
As if tears of grief had been crystalized,
salt preserved the dead. Without salt, meals
become an exercise in bas-relief.
I love you more than salt, the wise girl told
her foolish, fond old father before he
banished her. A pillar of the gastro-
nomical community, this holy
rock rocks the world. Is it wrong to lick
a Pringle bare? Is salaciousness
a sin if a pinch of concupiscence
is the only condiment I need?

IV: Eggs and that chicken business

Eggs. The supernovae of the kitchen,
the sunshine states, the principalities.

All that is is inside looking in. A protein-
fest to bond and bind and gelatinize;

when unyoked from itself, albumen beaten
to mountain peaks. As a woman, you also

know the pre-programmed ovarian
descent, how much is given in the forming.

For chickens, the journey begins with light,
a cue. Daylight or artifice—sadly

for the bird's sake it doesn't matter which.
That's why we imprison these mothers with ease

and make them lay as if all light is kin
to enlightenment, as if the dark is only uterine.

V: Mushrooms and other symbionts

Mushrooms are a lot like Emily D:
in their dark necropoles they preach death,
insinuate cupolas—aborigines
whose antediluvian gills and pores
translate the subtle earth. Mycorrhizal
fungi may be our new plastic, but old
acumen is what you taste, antiphonal
call and response, the psilocybin underworld.

As if pried from ghostly coral reefs,
these marrow fellows in the grass, these fairy-
circle* colonists, are parasitic
philanthropists, masters of the catalytic
relationship of each to each...or maybe
only this: nature's way of hugging trees.

---

*   Rings of seemingly dead foliage around mushroom clusters are said to testify to the existence of fairies, who (not being light-footed, one assumes) danced in those areas.

Sense and Sensitivity

Without your English sensibility you would never
       have been so sensible. You wore your gender like a woman

      at a masquerade—with a playful sense of irony.
Your heroines strolled between the hedgerows

at a genteel distance from where the wild things are.
       You played Truth and Consequences with the hungry spinster

      whose story heretofore in all the tomes of consequence
had been inconsequential.

The English in you made you pour the tea
       the Jane in you made you run your finger

      along the barely perceptible crack in the cup
and point out the bone in the china.

Beneath a cultivated reticence and artful sensitivity
       you dared to suggest the discursive dance of the blade

      as it pruned the Regency garden, trained the bushes
to miniaturization, and clipped (not quite) the earth's spontaneous, beating wings.

Custodians of the Bush

Fifteen feet above my head the effrontery of the bush:
on my roof of corrugated tin, corpses were being flung—
or toddler-sized bags of rice, or paunchy parachutists in stilettos.

Africa was a few days old from my perspective; I was still a Catholic.
Colored was *Black* again in the fists of Americans, but I
was a refugee, chastened by London's pale tribes.

My malaria-pill nightmare had sweated me awake but it was this
unscheduled visitation that finally slaughtered sleep.
Under the mosquito net the virgin I was then debated her next move.

Reason made me brave: monkeys, most likely—
not death raining down upon me. (Back then,
rape was not the most popular jock in school,

children hadn't yet been taught to sever their neighbors' hands;
diamonds were still the Eastern Province's BFF; Chuck Taylor
wasn't yet the anti-Christ; and one-party states were all the rage.)

This virgin crossed herself to ward off violation as vestal virgins do
and crept outside. Just past dawn and pot-bellied children were scurrying
to work. The pot-holed road that ran beneath my martyrdom

reared up like a stallion and kicked me in the crotch.
Foreign Virgin, the bush yelled—its accent flavored
with a soupçon of genocide—*what the hell are you doing here?*

A grubby goat was tethered to a nearby post, its crusty eyes
bulging in dismay, its bleating urgent as a jackhammer.
I saw them then, lined up like soldiers—the jungle's janitors,

the bush's last word in jurisprudence.
From the safety of my roof, a trinity of vultures
eyed the goat and me like shoppers peering at an expiration date.

Hungry, humorless generals
all they had to do
was wait.

I hurried back inside and held my breath for two years
in the sauna of the tropics. On Sundays and on Holy Days
of Obligation I trotted to church.

I taught the excised village girls
to explicate *Macbeth*,
how not to explicate a virgin.

I grew accustomed to the birds'
ungainly dance; the click of their scalpel
claws lulled me back to sleep.

I forgot the goat (not devoured by the trinity
after all but by the missionaries) and lived the way expatriates live
in the bush, with one beady eye on an exit.

Creatures of blinkered sentience, the bush's
winged custodians become the archangels of hygiene.
We, on the other hand, who kill to kill, have always known

no bones we toss aside
can ever be picked
clean.

Severing Ties (for fun)
For NG and VF

The Ties of the Boardroom	Ties Worn by Wayward Women
Thin landing strips of	Saucy usurpations as
tolerance; absurdist	pointy as witches'
gestures to the	hats; contrauntal
seasons; muted	commentary—di-
exclamation	dactic, impera-
points; the	tive, bold;
motley fools	anecdotal
of a ubiqui-	catalysts;
tous gray	alliances
army; ser-	with the
pents of	middle
haute-	finger;
cou-	radical
ture;	tamings;
tribal	inaliena-
Band-	ble pro-
aids	clamations
worn	against
over	the ty-
hearts	ranny
that	of all
yearn	te-
to	the-
beat	rings

I Don't Dance Much Anymore
For L

I used to dance like someone who knew
that movement embraced by ethnicity
was a fundamental trope of light and dark.
I don't dance much anymore even though I'm
biracial so it's half-expected. I don't sing
much either, though the bathtub or shower
can fake me into a glissando of notes that come
from somewhere I used not to be ashamed of.
Or I'm out with friends and we launch into *The Sound
of Music* or *Porgy and Bess* because some of us
know all the words, and some of us are black
and/or gay, and we *do* have confidence in we
for the time being, and the summertime *is* liltingly easy
to coast through. It's then that me (singing) and you
(listening) are like dragonflies riding the warm swell
of the air the way we used to ride each other when
sacramental love was always on the menu.

I've read this over and it sounds as if, after two
decades, my love for you has dimmed. Granted,
it's not as videotape-able as it used to be
but that's because performance is dependent
on the insertion of perspective—a pushing away,
an observation of the self-outside-the-selves.
How can that be done when your self and mine
are indivisible? If you die before me, I will lie
with you each night, my shadow-lover, my perfusive ghost,
as we cavort in winding sheets. Your voice
(which never could hold a tune) will minister to me.
Distance won't have a word to say for itself.
Space will be our shroud, and love alone,
my private apparition, will serve as requiem.

CHILDREN'S CANTICLES

I: Texting: A Ballad for Children

the girl is always taptaptap
in bed at church at meals
the morse code of her tapping thumbs
is how she knows she's real

texting is a lot like sex
though she knows it isn't nice
to participate in gang rapes
she doesn't take advice

from those outside her group of girls
who cannot know the tribe
and don't wear the fontal war paint
of the other scribes

her mother tries to intercede
and takes the thing away
the girl looks up with eyes of dust
you're killing me she says

the mother gives it back at last
her daughter's in despair
she's cut a hundred perfect holes
in jeans she liked to wear

the holes resemble mouths of ghosts
or agony or rage
the mother cannot look at them
her daughter's in a cage

tonight the war dance of the thumbs
is turning girls' rooms red
LoladoubleD is doomed
they're lopping off her head

Lola's quite a hefty dish
as meaty as strip steak
the girl cannot deny herself
she's obliged to masticate

skank! and *ho!* and *fat!* and *bitch!*
can't help but titillate
and now that it's in writing
there's nothing to debate

the word is god the word is said
the word can filet dreams
the texterettes have thumbs of steel
they've just excised a queen

the girl feels something like remorse
Lola was her friend
but friendship doesn't matter here
and everything must end

she taps out tunes in the minor key
with the stubby white canes of her thumbs
she feels a tether holding her
she yearns to cut and run

and late at night her mother hears
her daughter's frenzied taps
and knows she's in a place devoid
of tenderness and maps

the girl is always taptaptap
it's how she knows she's real
the pain on the pads of her aching thumbs
the only thing she feels

II: Childhood Garden: Battersea, South London
For TR

Eden it wasn't. A bomb shelter at one end left over from the Blitz, a patch
of insipid grass more stubble than lawn, neighbours' windows squinting
over dank walls, a rusty swing grinding its grubby anthem to the sky,
Mum's threadbare underwear sighing on the washing line

or maybe this instead…

a swing to swing me low sweet chariot
to the sun and moon and back again
a pendulum of smiles
or maybe flowers so reticent they could only
be seen with a magnifying glass and sanguinity
or maybe fairies too Mum said (not dreaming of coffins today)
or maybe there was pleasure to be found in the adulterous
undulation of underwear and the exquisite gyrations
of nighties and knickers and darned socks
a singular goddam joy to unravel
inside the modus operandi of kinesis
or maybe there was a mischievous snake
and a green apple after all
a naked woman hungry for a nakeder man
an abandoned fig leaf or two…(yes there were two)
and organ music as well gushing up
from the bowels of the earth like Big Oil

and maybe in the garden's center—its navel— was a tree
heavy-breasted with fruit, fertilized and fecund
and standing for something entirely and indubitably

and not belonging to anyone.

III: Primary Circles

Nothing about me says *welfare* now unless
I want it to. Back then my mouth betrayed me
as clearly as the incline on the heels
of my shoes, brought about by a tendency
I had to place my weight on the outer edges
of my feet, as if I were a skater
about to make a turn. I learned how not
to smile. Like my shoes, my chipped, vampire
teeth were liabilities. On London
asphalt, without a blade of grass in sight,
I hid my soiled school tie, squirmed in my skirt
of grubby pleats. When two dozen girls
surrounded me I assumed I was
the Farmer in his Den. The little girls
held hands in a stolid, ancient circle.
I scanned the circle like a fool looking
for a friend to play my wife. But that day
I wasn't the farmer after all. That day
I was the Brown Girl in the Ring. When the slow chant
began (*"Wog! Wog!"*) I smiled nervously,
forgot to hide my ugly broken teeth.
It was the spontaneity of the dance
that frightened me. For if little white girls
could rouse themselves without warning, what good
were the shields I'd procured for myself—my fine
vocabulary, my careful accent,
my "A's" in English, the knack I had for drawing
portraits of hungry girls to give away
as bribes? What good such amelioration
against these eight-year-olds' impromptu savagery?
I willed myself blind and deaf and dumb.
I was clutching something small—a book perhaps—
the only external detail that refuses
to accost me. I'd known the rage of *nigger,*
coon, monkey, and *wog* before, but not

the synchronized animus of white girls
at play.
            Decades later, I smile with the
majority. When I picture the circle
now I'm not a brown girl frozen
to its hub. Instead, I clutch
to my small chest whatever it is
I have in my hand (a book, perhaps,
or misery, or a borrowed knife)
and walk right through the girls as if they're nothing
more than ghosts. The little girls with ribbons
in their hair watch me go. I turn to see
their fingers and their ribbons are unfurled.
Time has undone them. When I glance back
they are waving or applauding—their guilty
ribbons flutter on their heads like pretty
pastel tapeworms. I tell them I am not
afraid to love them. I tell them I am
not afraid of their contagious fear.
I smile at my white best friend who leaps right out
of the circle to come and hold my hand. I open
up to a scream. Out fly teeth from a fixed
mouth—white maggots cocooned in songs
of sorrow, honed as sharp as a knife.

Madonna in the Bush

A woman carries water on her head.
The way she moves is function's nod to form.
Watching her I know what I once knew:
walking is as close to god as prayer.
The bush around us pulses, swirls, and falls
as energy and matter paint the dark.

Unnatural is the soul who fears the dark
when shadows are a habit of the head.
That which propels us to rising has to fall.
What is there to see with if not form?
Uncertainty's a principle of prayer
and *Beauty* is a word I thought I knew....

Strange how we lose the things we knew
and reinvent the subject in the dark.
Observation is an alternate path to prayer
but who can escape the clamor in the head
when all sight is seen, all beauty bound to form?
Beauty is the way a bare foot falls

on a dust-blush path in the bush where fall
is as distant as mirrors, and a woman knows
the weight of the child on her back—his form
conforming to hers, his dark their dark.
The word for *mother* beats inside her head.
Motherhood is devotion—this the prayer.

Need and wish and hope give birth to prayer.
We brace ourselves against the pull of fall.
The woman carrying water on her head
perceives a world the likes of me can't know.
Balance is to movement what shadow is to dark—
the only words worth knowing are the ones we form.

The busy world I live in seems devoid of form
and migration is the route I take from prayer.
I forget to wonder what's inside the dark—
a body falling can't perceive the fall.
Yet I believe there's something mothers know
holier than the noise inside my head:

a woman's form can alchemize the fall
and prayer is sight's homage to what is known—
beauty dark enough to balance light upon its head.

Another Summer

Today in Southwest Virginia the earth bends like a butler and offers me
tranquility on a golden tray. Sunlight turns color into soul food.

Today's so goddam *bright*—a sequin shimmer, a face bereft
of shadow, an orchestra of tiny yellow butterflies,

an amber brooch pinned to a giggle of cerulean,
and the quiet green sleeve of grass in my yard

mowed by a man I've loved for more than twenty years.
The beatific buzz saw of summer has felled me all over again.

Later, light will be an old nun, bashfully slipping in and out
and in between, her motion betraying a tender familiarity with dusk.

But for now, dropped into stained glass, I dissolve
like Alka-Seltzer. If I die on this day it will be an apotheosis—

an unsheathing from the scabbard of the self, a small heat rising
to the clamor of yellow wings churning the air, and fat funereal worms

tilling the warm ripe earth around me in readiness.

Narrative Arcs in Hindsight

I have been fed into the circular saw of the moon by another's
turbulence. But the principal cause for concern is Jarrell's "90 North,"
where pain doesn't amount to wisdom,
it only amounts to pain—

a cold-blue apex where meaninglessness and suffering are conjoined—
a refutation of the classic tales that led you to the top
of the hill then led you back down again
denouement-ally, the way a parent puts a child to bed.

In the story-shadow trailing ahead, the arc becomes a scythe in Act III,
raking across my 1st-person point of view the way a Glock—
that furious cousin of parallax—raped the point of view
I imagined I'd held for 50 years.

The setting moves from Jarrell's climactic
cold to William Duffy's pretty farm in Pine Island, Minnesota
where James the Right rocks hammocks. *I have not wasted my life*, I insist,
pinning wax butterflies to Jim's suicidal sky.

The older I get the more I believe in relationships—the one between
the writer and the thoughts of other writers, for example, or the one
between the maternal and the future—a rare constant that reproduces
constancy. Though sad men may seduce, the need to reply with "there is

more than this I know" is also fundamental. The arc isn't a covenant
with others, it's a covenant with the self in its universal disguise.
We're all gods of the inter-dependent clause. Maybe the secret is
that the moment must function both as climax *and* as point of view.

After so much loss I still believe—still want to believe tonight—
that the Small-Life we weave can dance a cosmos.

Fabric

I sewed like a daredevil when I was young—made my first
wedding dress from satin polyester as white as daVinci Veneers.
I even hand-embroidered a frenzy of pastel flowers on the collar
and the sleeves. Sewing a wedding gown is to dressmaking
what Nascar is to driving—risky. I don't sew much anymore.
13 years later, I bought my second wedding dress in Greensboro,
North Carolina. It was the color of clotted cream, a snug sheath
of beaded lace. A man shopping with his wife said, *Even Brother Ray*
would love how you look in that, Sister, which sealed the deal.
But after it was altered one of the seams was as crooked as a broken
finger. Accustomed to making room for error, I said nothing, positioned
my large bouquet of gardenias just so to hide it. My wedding florist,
a man called Mr. Tickle, had saved the day. Comedy wins out in the end.
Tension is the pressure placed upon the bobbin and the needle;
speed is dictated by the right foot. Too much tension, too much speed
and everything is ruined—which is why for two decades I've been meaning
to sew a sari-length of silk into a blouse—a gift from friends who lived in India.
The color of a bruised sunrise, the material is artfully female—
a hose-sheer sendal, a lewd mousseline, a diaphanous pellicule
to be wound around my bare brown body like a lover
or a shroud. Every few years when I open that drawer the exclamatory
fabric prods me towards ambition. I make plans to dust off my vintage
Montgomery Ward sewing machine, score the fabric with tailor's chalk,
domesticate it with pinking shears, blind-hem stitch it, and reinforce
its raw edges with zig-zag goose-steps. But its leafy silver emblems
make me nervous. They are too finished; they shimmer seductively
against a pensive purple and whisper in the language of warp and weft.
Next year (or the year after) I will hear the sari-length of fabric
mouthing its operatic chorus from inside my bottom drawer.
I will locate it in the dark with tall hands. Fearless, I won't fudge the seams
or crucify the buttonholes. Its colors will be colorfast, its silver will never tarnish.
As the purple river plucks the thinnest strings of silver from the stars,
I'll trace its weighty undulations and think how hard it is to baste ourselves
to time and place, all the while praying for permanence to take hold.

PART III: American Angelus: An Immigrant's Ode

Oh, say does that star-spangled banner yet wave
O'er the land of the free and the home of the brave?

Orogeny*

Beyond the field behind the house, beyond
North Main and all around this old New River
Valley the Appalachians rise, seismic's
two-hundred-and-fifty-million-year-old
tectonic odometers. Ridged molars
take their usual bite out of the blue.
Before roads, before maps, before landscape
ushered in perspective, before sentience
instilled pathetic fallacy, these mountains
stood. Once taller than the Rockies, their peaks
eroded from majesty to modesty.
As far as we know, Earth is the only place
in the entire solar system with linear
mountain ranges. Before sight was tempered
by new-found relativity, the first
men and women saw them—these ranges
helped define omniscience, encouraged us
to shed our first-person limited point
of view. Gods are found on mountain tops.
Without these peaks, horizons are bound to soil;
with them, the giddy splendor of escalation,
the faith-engendering topography of *always*.

---

* The process of mountain formation.

Laura Nyro, American Queen

sang the way Hepburn walked in trousers.
In our mobile-home-sized maisonette in the refugee
section of Black-British Brixton, Laura's confidence
was beads of sweat and Christmas.
Her American-Jewish-Italian blues
taught us how to groove smooth—
soothed our beating hearts before
she shattered them again.

Lay me down, Laura. Lay me down in your palace
of broken eggs.* Your tongue is a flame,
your full-lipped chalice of pain the one child
born again inside your throat.

You refused to seek sanctuary
in someone else's heaven. Had you stopped
by on your way from New York
to solitude I would've married you, Laura—
been eager to picnic, happy to get stoned.

Lay me down, Laura. Lay me down in your palace
of broken eggs. Your tongue is a flame,
your full-lipped chalice of pain the one child
born again inside your throat.

Each time it's the same. The stylus clears
its throat on the black, consecrated circle
to signal the start of the mass.
The way you sang was how a not-yet-born child
births itself. Breath is a baby's body-length
away down a narrow, pulsing causeway—
and though the road can strangle as easily
as liberate, the egg-song is the only thing
worth dying for, the one child who demands to be born.

---

*   Singer-songwriter Laura Nyro died of ovarian cancer in 1997.

The Femalien: a Performance Manifesto
For TM

She's an exaltation of estrogen, a flock of mud birds
She lands on rooftops, congregates in the boughs of rambunctious trees

She's observant: on sorties to the well She
notes how the world shivers on a shifting plane

She's been trained to walk without letting
a drop of what is precious fall

She's a crescendo of locusts
from a land of wind-driven splendor

She hovers at the exits to museums
infests library books and writes in blood: *Birth. Death. Longing.*

But when the burqa of weary blues
with its woven portcullis

of a viewing screen is lifted, She'll fly out like a queen singing,
O, honey, it's been too long a-comin'

rising with the consistency of hearty yeasty
wholesome wheaty bread to feed the famished world

STILL LIFE with Violence

I: Stealth

The fontanel over Blacksburg is as innocent and baby-blue
as the Tar Heels' helmets. On the field is an emblem of remembrance—
a maroon *VT* lashed to an orange ribbon.

Ambush has left allegory in its wake. The new logo is fixed
to lapels and painted onto fields of green.
Since April, it's become a kind of Hokie crucifix.

At noon, the B-2 Spirit Stealth Bomber zooms overhead
like the tab on a zipper. The sky fractures.
I'm not at the game today; I'm home nursing an injury.

Safer that way. Contact can be dangerous.
But I can't escape the delayed roar of the bird of prey
as it flies over my house en route to glory.

It's the sound of war suspended, an audacious audible,
the sound men of war make before they go to battle.
On the way to a football game years ago, Stealth flew right over us.

We looked up and saw the belly of a bat or a pterodactyl—
so close we could see its absence of pores, its brooding capability.
Its angles were pitiless, its wings as resolute as edicts.

It crept up on us like a spy, made us scream. Shocked and awed
that the military's favorite mascot had accosted us, we stared
at wings sculpted by giant pinking shears.

Today, the fans look up to see the machine hurtling towards them.
Knowing what's coming, the stadium shudders. But against North Carolina
(1 and 3 in the ACC), we have the ammo to win.

Orange and maroon leaves flutter toward their inevitable suicide.
The leaves underfoot are as fragile as the bones of baby birds.
I can't look up to see them fall.

II: On the Syllabus Today: Blue Skies

Today I awake sizzling with hope—determined
to teach something that can't be undermined

I'm an elder of sorts, passing into the age of wisdom.
Today everything I say will emphasize viability

I will be emphatic but not orthodox—I will plough the land
of post-apocalyptic post-adolescence like a farmer or a priest

Inside the class-confessional, beside the mournful furrows
of the earth, we won't ask each other awkward questions

like what does *rampage* mean?
History will not simmer—we will not be surprised

Inside in the bald cupola of Virginia Tech's Green Zone
youth will look at me with eyes wide open

Beyond the classroom windows' polite geometry, things
tunnel up through the earth—renegade poppies

But today I will direct the eyes of youth upwards
I will point to the sky's bland immensity of blue

the only point of view elders dare pass on
to their vibrant vulnerable young

III: A Mind Full of Winter

Violence, sleep's serial killer, has the patience of a saint.
You stay up late to fool him—2 or 3 AM…later, even.
For months you've been dodging bullets but the disc is stuck on repeat:
soon, when you're most vulnerable, he'll murder you again.
However much you fight it you will eventually fall asleep.
Here we are on Main Street about to board a jumbo jet.
As usual, we're boarding as meekly as lambs, without bandages
or anti-depressants, without an exit plan.
Copters hover overhead—motorized guardian angels.
Come down to earth and save us! someone pleads. But the town
is trapped inside the snow globe inside a young man's head. Someone's
forgotten to load our luggage but someone else in the seat beside us
has remembered to load his guns. Air marshal? Outlaw? Student?
Our generous wingspan dictates a runway, but we surprise everyone
with an early take-off along Main Street—the buildings on either side
beheaded by the jumbo's urgent wings—residents, too.
As sirens beat the crap out of the pastoral
we glide into a brute blue sky, aim for the eye of the bull.
From the air, Blacksburg is Toy Town. In the blink of an eye,
post-attack, post-traumatic Tech's on TV, dressed in mourning.
Hurtling into consciousness you engage in semantic self-help:
Place the kid in context; research his sly x/y coordinates
to find out where he's been. ("x" is springtime tilted towards winter;
"y" a violation of space.) The graph of consolation is not a consolation
prize. So tonight, having taught your graduate class the gentler forms
of theory, you exhume a poet and put him on the witness stand
even though he saw nothing. Mr. Wallace Stevens takes the Fifth
but still you pummel him with questions: *Is it a cliché*
if the boy in the dream turns into a Snowman?
And is this supple, turbulent thing a devil or a detail?
If the knocking is for me, his professor, should I open my office door
mid-flight to let him in? And, if the tomb is closed and the stone
unmoved, is new chaos inescapable and crusted with snow?
Last but not least, how will I bear the Nothing there is if I don't get
out of this goddamn burning plane, and soon?

Meanwhile, on the dark side of the sepulcher, Seung-Hui Cho,
a boy with a mind full of winter, does his nightly run
to Main Street's post office to mail his death-discs to NBC.
As usual in this episode the boy with the gun is a metaphor,
the gun with the boy is, too.

Imagery always wins, says the Snowman.
Imagery is mine, says the boy.

IV: CSI: Virginia Tech (A 32-line Elegy)

Here among the fractured, it's all about paying
attention. No clue is too small.
Years after the slaying the community speaks
with the circumspection of a cop or a mortician.
You (the residual pronoun who taught
the shooter) strive to make amends.

Preoccupied not with whodunits—
you know that—but with why and how
it was done you take your eye off
the here and now—a swarm of yellow
jackets descending from ceiling tiles.
Another plague made personal.

You raise the alarm. Men from Physical Plant
arrive on the scene with pesticides.
Favoring repetition, they spray and spray.
Soon you have a hundred dead and dying
on your windowsill. Your office turns into a morgue.
You sit behind your desk in your little shop of horrors.

Colleagues offer condolences. Since the mass
shooting of 32 you're on a quest for silver linings.
You tell them, "These creatures are merciful—
they buzz before they strike." But the insects triumph,
wear you down. You're forced to relocate
to an office on the other side of the hall—a foreign country.

You creep back at intervals,
scoop the little corpses
off the sill and drop them
into Tupperware containers
brought from home.
You count them all forensically—
these bodies curved by death into commas,
insinuating that the sentence will never be done.

V: End Words: A Sestina

Spring or fall it's a solemn story: Seung—
hungry, chimerical, his sunglasses
winking in the room's pale light, his sorrow
sinking us both, as if our shoes are stone
tablets and the carpet is mud—waits. Silence
expands like a lung. Cho is under the gun.

Two years later, at the range, the gun
teaches a new lesson about holes. Seung
likes the histrionic bullets. Silent
behind his ostentatious sunglasses
he wills himself to turn soft flesh to stone.
He must kill soon. An unkempt sorrow

blooms, spreads its wings. He waits till sorrow
flies clean away. He's confident with guns—
spent years telling himself that sticks and stones
may break his bones but words can never...Seung
mutes the volume on the world, his sunglasses
doing with light what his sermonic silence

does with speech. The sovereignty of silence
hems him in. His catechism, sorrow,
sat between us when we met. His sunglasses
thrust me onto glass. He did not bring guns
with which to shoot me. I don't know why. Seung
brought me gifts instead: ponderous stones

to hang around my neck—a dull, whetstone
rosary. In April, pumping silence
full of expletives, the Riddle-Boy, Seung—
his own wounds now encrypted, his sorrow
gorged and frantic—brandished a pair of guns,
removed—forever—his sunglasses.

I was a teacher; now I wear sunglasses.
Sight is kinder on a dimmer switch. Headstones
bruise me. (*Sorrow, sorrow everywhere, only salt to drink.*) The gun
tells time—click-Glock, click-Glock. Kindly voices
give us CPR: "Sever horror from beauty,"
they warn.
           By their laughter I know my students

hear the voices of an unarmed choir. We teach
peace in the stuttering light, reconcile silence
with the world's residual, clamorous beauty.

Old Masters

after W. H. Auden's "Musée des Beaux Arts"

About poetry he is never wrong.
The old master adjusts his tie, says,
The poetry of protest is dead.
The essay is the forum for politics

Not in the ballroom is a young man tied to a tree.
His scrotum is being adjusted. About men
he is never wrong: old masters with epitaphic hands.
Don't kill me! he begs
until they do

Wax wings blister and melt. Something—
small from this angle—plops into the sea.
Location
location
location.

Venus Genetrix

In April, she thinks of her mother, who died on that first day
of fools. Her mom liked cats. Venus inherited them.
As a joke, she renamed them Anchises and Adonis.
No one got it. When she's got nothing better to do
she rubs their little pot bellies, counts their purrs. Contact
with the living helps her avoid murdering something. Her ex
was no lover. His passions were excessive moderation and
Fruit Loops. As soon as Ralph was satisfied he'd come
to an abrupt halt, as if he'd run into a stop sign inside
what he called her "love canal." After five years,
Ralph ran away to a town in the top left-hand corner of Idaho.
For eight years and counting, Venus's ring finger has been available
for lease. At the bank, the chorus refers to her as eccentric.
She knows that's a lie. She took a test and was found to be 99%
normal. The chorus spreads rumors, glances over at her—
motorists rubber-necking at road kill. Apart from reruns of *Sex
and the City*, there's not a scrap of romance left in her life.
In her tutu-like ensemble, Carrie Bradshaw gazes up at New York,
a city where the phallic taunts of men are made manifest
in glass, concrete, and steel. During the final episode, the four
hungry women are getting laid regularly by men who pay
no attention to road signs. The message rubs like a hair shirt:
Have faith and you will find Him. At night, Mr. Big,
heavy as the Empire State, moves urgently above her—
Mars and Venus in a retrograde rotation.
All over the city, men are riding into other women's
vaginal sunsets. But a love goddess must think positively or die:
she's only 800 million years old and still as hot as hell.
With false fingernails Vee clings to a shaft of hope
and slips down his skyscraper-ry spine, nails gouging bloody
channels into his flesh. "What's your name, Beautiful?" he asks,
naïve as a codfish, a permanent drifter. Or is it the city
doing the asking? She's not sure. Either way, she smiles,
and gives her imaginary friend her stage name: "It's Lucifer,"
she says, rising. "Shall we go again?"

Fear of Blindness on a Summer Morning

As that bitch Blindness yaps at your heels
another bowl of color for breakfast
in an eye-shaped spoon.
Use it to shovel in the sky
with your Special K.

The sky is rimmed with stainless steel—
alleluia-blues teaspooned, hues calculated.
Color receptors on overload, radiation
within the visible spectrum.
Swallow the eye candy whole.

This miraculous refraction of light
a pact with god. Another, more personal—
to let you keep your sight a while longer.
You can still see clearly.
A million nerve fibers
busily at work. The eyes don't see
anyway; the brain does. All eyes do
is collect the info. All you need to do
is learn how to retrieve it in the dark.

Meanwhile, stop whining
and dare to keep looking—
dare to remember the view.

Redshift

I'm afraid you're moving away from me
the shift can happen at the speed of light
your world expands, allows more space to be

love is not stasis, love is energy
you think you may and then I think I might
I'm afraid you're moving away from me

love—cosmological constant or fascimile?
please don't turn away, I rarely bite
your world expands, allows more space to be

we're increasingly convinced it's ennui
that makes us careful, overly polite
I'm afraid you're moving away from me

bodies in love are like mass and gravity
dark energy's a void, a parasite
your world expands, allows more space to be

love doesn't come with a warranty
the medium for love is appetite
I'm afraid you're moving away from me
my world contracts, allows more space to be

To Racism

In recognition of the looming extinction
as prison-for-profit marched
our next millionth man to jail,
we took matters into our own hands,

propelled you to the nearest
dumpster and threw you in.
We were sick to death of you
peeking out from under white, connotative

sheets, trying to play the invisible man.
We would have rid ourselves of you for good
if it hadn't been for all that whimpering.
A good Samaritan (a lawyer, I think)

reached in, sewed you up as tight as pigskin,
and siphoned you back out onto the streets.
When I saw you again in the furtive
shadows you were cradling a black doll

like the one Daddy bought for me.
I swear I thought you'd had a come-to-Jesus
moment—til I looked harder and saw
your Mickey-Mouse minstrel-gloves,

blackface slathered on as thick as Hershey's....
And then the crow cawed and I
heard twin sockets shrieking
where the doll's eyes should have been.

And this poem is familiar to people who don't read
poetry, who don't know it's not supposed to work
like this...which is why I wrote it,
which is why it will be read.

American Angelus: An Immigrant's Ode

I: Sunrise
More than a decade into a new millennium, I am lying
in bed with you, America, as you grumble about the pea

under the mattress. *What can I say?* you tell me,
You know I've always been sensitive. And this one's so green.

You pose on our queen-sized bed, adjust your sunburst tiara,
flutter your long-as-a-sermon eyelashes.

Sunlight streams through the hole we punched in the ceiling
to gaze at the parchment moon after one too many single malts.

Time honks his horn like a horny homeboy. We ignore the old fart.
We're insider trading under our Martha Stewart sheets

in the whirl of a tense present, whipping up sex into cupcakes.
My love is as lusty as Margaret's Scarlett, as reticent as

Hawthorne's Hester, as precocious as Shirley's temple.
All ringlets and apple pie, my idol demands second helpings

lives (on and off) by a creed written by wise men who wrote Liberty
on tall paper before the South could read.

Over breakfast, you remind me of the politics of compromise.
"When politics screws ideology, morality's a condiment," I point out.

We're all going to hell in a hand basket, hon, she says.
Shut up and pass the salt.

I place my Negro-colored-Black-Afro-Caribbean-African-American-
without-the-hyphen-Biracial-immigrant hand inside yours, America,

which is more coppery green than white and slippery as an idea.
I swim around inside your palm, a little brown fish. *My mulatto,*

you croon, not meaning to offend, *my little brown pea.* Your peals
of laughter rise like prayer-bubbles, tolling for us both.

Every morning it's the same aubade—you reciting your riddle-creed:
Every day is garbage day. We must trash

what we need, keep the rest. Everyone collects something
they yearn to throw away. How else could God have been invented?

In fact (you rub your pea-green eyes) *the space-time matrix*
is an unreliable narrator. The future rushes by us

out of breath and crabby in her high heels—Lady Gaga on speed.
We march onwards down the little Lady's birth canal.

You have eyes wide enough to see through a punched-out sky-
light into other galaxies, a mind large enough to sieve parallel universes

from the detritus. And I love to suckle at your ginormous breasts,
my Whitmanic, incomparable, arrogant, crass, idiot-savant angel,

my electric-alchemic Muse, my land of the found and the ready
to be ready-made, my totemic untenable circumference.

Beloved America, pinup girl and queen—
my triple Hail Mary, my lover, my dream....

II: High Noon

Directly above us   the din of midday
Shit-scared and disgruntled   I gaze through the skylight
You are still snoring   you're older now, weepy
your Seagram's beside you   your summer read lusty
Hope-hoarding and hapless   a gullible dreamer
Called to prayer-song   but distracted by pixels
Screens soon enchant you   seductive and simple
Soap-opera starlits   hunks strapping and bland-faced
The climax is killing   as kennings whiz by us

Colt-strong and Glock-sturdy   cowboys and gladiators
Whose bullets sing love songs   to all the dead virgins
Bells battle for victory   you cover your ears
War is alliterative   war wounds the wounded
In your dreams there are ballads   someone is crooning
A king shuffles eastward   a son plays a knight
And noon is a notion   as high as a kite....

The sky is white; the world spills into noon.
You smile. All love is close to prayer;
and the mercy of the angelus
abides in the taut promise of its bells,
the way they arouse the soul, their ringing
an awakening to lyric and to death.

This country of old men flirts with death
as the sun pins itself to white at noon
as if white were a cause. The ringing
in our ears is nothing like a prayer.
You yearn for the solace of the bell's
curve but something fell through the angelus

and got stuck on the other side. *The angel? Us?*
Mary? you can't tell. You are sick of death,
the way it secretes itself between the bell's
wide lips, the way it translates noon
into something sooner. The call to prayer
is an obsession, a stubborn ringing

in your ears. If this blasted ringing
doesn't stop we'll go mad. The angelus
can't belong to you. It's not a prayer
well suited to a land where sex and death
play chess with each other at noon.
Deafness and dogma doled out in decibels.

You, my love, desire climax. *Ring my bell,*
you plead. I do. But my clumsy ringing
is not a worthy entry into the afternoon.
Something insidious about the angelus
holds us in like spandex. A little death
sprinkled like salt (or maybe ash) on prayer

tames our libidos. The Credo—a prayer
you learned in your youth—never lets lust's bells
ring for long. All sounds march to death
and all the clay gods made in school ring
the same cracked bell. The midday angelus
re-conceives a virgin at the stroke of noon.

But death is never a virgin and passion engenders prayer.
Noon cracks open like a skull under a guillotine of bells
while inside the confessional, a choir of washer women wring out the angelus.

III: Sunset Orison

Your stones proclaim la petite mort
their shadows verse and psalm
Your swinging trees are sermons
do no harm, do no harm, do no harm

We walk a gender into night
We eat upon the ground
We will not lie inside a tomb
hooded and without sound

The mouth of the South keeps moving
the eyes of the South are red
ears in the South still waltzing
to the tunes of the boys long dead

The kettle whistles Dixie, and the landscapes chant the red rhythms
of lost tribes. In the South and the North we're all cross-bred.

O, America, I have been listening from my new perch
unseen in the rusting glory-cage of the South.

You are not yet old. Your fingers are still green.
And what of the bells of sunset? What of the prayer of dust?

The bell is the mouth that dares, still, to open.
The prayer, my love, is us.

END NOTES

My thanks to the humanitarian organization CARE for inviting me to be part of a small delegation of women to Sierra Leone in 2010 to study maternal and infant health and report our findings to 10 Downing Street. Several poems in the collection were written as a result of that visit.

"Cordon Sanitaire." In August 2014, following Ebola outbreaks in Liberia, Guinea, and Sierra Leone, cordons were established around infected areas. Until the outbreak was thought to be contained, no one was allowed to leave. It was the first time cordons had been established in nearly a century. The last was during a typhus outbreak in 1918.

"Making Progress." Graham Greene's famous novel *The Heart of the Matter* is set in Sierra Leone.
--*Plumpy'Nut* is a ready-to-use therapeutic food in a packet. Designed in 1996 by Nutriset and the French Institute of Research and Development, it is used to treat malnutrition and has saved countless lives. It can be stored for two years without refrigeration.
--Kabala is the capital of the Koinadugu District in the Northern Province of Sierra Leone. Remote and beautiful, it is very hard to reach without helicopter transportation, particularly during the rainy season.

"1x4: A War Requiem." Many of the war poems were written following trips back to post-war Sierra Leone in 2006/2007 and 2010. The war began in 1991 and peace was established in 2002, following UN and British forces' intervention. I taught as a VSO in Lunsar from 1977-79.

"Diamonds in the rough." The RUF (Revolutionary United Front) was a guerilla unit that killed 50,000 people, maimed thousands more, and displaced millions in Sierra Leone. Their primary source of funding was alluvial diamonds. They were notorious for recruiting child soldiers and committing atrocities. Their leader was Foday Saybana Sankoh, an ally of Charles Taylor and his National Patriotic Front of Liberia.

"Detention & Multiplication." G3 rifles are manufactured in Germany. They were widely utilized during the war in Sierra Leone.

"Our Waiter Wasn't Wounded." This cumulative-stanza, word-repeated tercet form is original, as far as I know. During the war in Sierra Leone, the horrifically casual question "Long sleeves or short sleeves?" was sometimes asked of victims prior to amputations.

"Ga Wree-Wre: The Judgment Mask." I am indebted to VMFA curators for the information provided about Ga Wree-Wre, and to the Library of Virginia for coordinating the project that resulted in a special poetry publication of poems written in response to works in the museum. I am also indebted to Professor Aneta Georgievska-Shine for her inspiring lecture on the relationship between art and literature, and Howell Perkins of the VMFA for his assistance with obtaining permission to use images of the African masks in this book.

--My father, writer and artist Namba Roy (1910-1961), was the Maroon carver for Jamaica. Born in the village of Accompong, he learned from his father how to call upon traditional African methods and symbols in his carvings. The Maroon carver tradition has been handed down from father to son since the 1700s.

--The Poro Society is a secret male society in West Africa. It wields significant authority in rural areas. The Bundu Society is the female equivalent of the Poro Society. These secret societies circumcise boys and excise girls in some rural regions of Sierra Leone.

"Love: A War Triangle." I was inspired by the excellent descriptions of these masks in *Selections from the Virginia Museum of Fine Arts* by Anne B. Barriault and Kay M. Davidson, University of Virginia Press.

"At the Aberdeen West African Fistula Center, Freetown." Obstetric fistula is readily treatable with surgery.

"Edible Sonnets I: Sea Vegetables." Sea vegetables are particularly vulnerable to heavy metal pollutants such as lead and arsenic.

--In the 1944 movie *Arsenic and Old Lace*, Cary Grant's screen aunts play charming homicidal maniacs.

"Edible Sonnets V: "Mushrooms & other symbionts." Psilocybin produces hallucinogenic effects for which mushrooms are famous.

"Custodians of the Bush." Excision or female circumcision is a common practice in many regions of Africa. In Sierra Leone, it is often performed by the members of female secret societies.

"Fabric." Certain fabrics are notoriously difficult to sew when they are very sheer.

"Still Life with Violence." This series of poems refers to the 2007 shooting rampage at Virginia Tech in which 32 faculty and students were murdered by student Seung-hui Cho, who committed suicide. While serving as Chair of English at Virginia Tech in 2005, I worked with and sought help for Cho.

"A Mind Full of Winter." Title from the first line of "The Snow Man" by Wallace Stevens.

--Following the shooting rampage at Virginia Tech, rescue helicopters had difficulty landing due to the unseasonably blustery weather.

"End Words: A Sestina." For an explanation of why I selected the sestina form for this poem see the chapter "A Boy Named Loser" in *No Right to Remain Silent: What We've Learned from the Tragedy at Virginia Tech* (Random House/Three Rivers Press).

"Venus Genetrix." Venus was said to be the mother of the Julian race of Caesars.

"Redshift." Redshift is "displacement of the spectrum of a celestial body toward longer wavelengths that is a consequence of the Doppler effect or the gravitational field of the source."—Merriam Webster.

"American Angelus: An Immigrant's Ode." The Angelus, the dawn, noon, and sunset prayer in celebration of the Incarnation and Annunciation, is often accompanied by the ringing of the angelus bell.

Though the majority of poems in this collection are written in open form, some inhabit prescribed or modified forms, including the following: Blank verse: "Lesson Number 1," "Orogeny," "Primary Circles." Blank verse variations: "*Ga Wree-Wre*: The Judgment Mask" and "Ngady amwaash Mask: His Sister, Mweel." Sestinas: "Madonna in the Bush," "End Words: A Sestina," and a buried sestina in "American Angelus: An Immigrant's Ode." Sonnets: (regular) "The Ceremony of the Dead, Sierra Leone," and from the sequence Edible Sonnets: (irregular) "Sea Vegetables," "Pasta: An Exegesis," "Salt," "Eggs—& that chicken business," "Mushrooms and other symbionts." Ballad stanzas: "Texting: A Ballad" and a buried ballad in "American Angelus: An Immigrant's Ode." Villanelles: "After Therapy, A Villanelle," "Redshift." Stitchic verse: "American Angelus: An Immigrant's Ode." Word-associative tercets: "Our Waiter Wasn't Wounded."

I am indebted to the following: Heather Buchanan (publisher) and Randall Horton (editor) at Aquarius Press/Willow Books; Jennifer Weltz, Jean Naggar, and the staff at the Jean V. Naggar Literary Agency; Helene Gayle, former President of CARE, and the CARE staff; the Library of Virginia and the Virginia Museum of Fine Arts; students I've taught in the U.K., Sierra Leone, and the U.S.; my friends and colleagues at Virginia Tech, whose work has so often inspired my own, and whose kindness has made Blacksburg home; my friends in the U.K., especially Tina Theis, Richenda Kullar, Denise Dowd, and the late Siobhan Dowd; my beloved family, particularly Joseph Roy-Stewart, Paula Robinson, Tamba Roy, and Gail Roy for their tireless support and encouragement; and Larry Jackson—my partner, my love, always.

About the Author

Lucinda Roy is an Alumni Distinguished Professor in Creative Writing at Virginia Tech where she teaches in the MFA program. Her awards include the Eighth Mountain Poetry Prize for *The Humming Birds*, a Discover Great New Writers selection from Barnes and Noble for her novel *Lady Moses*, and the Baxter Hathaway Poetry Prize for her slave narrative "Needlework." She received the Newsmaker of the Year award from the Virginia Press Women in recognition of her memoir *No Right to Remain Silent: What We've Learned from the Tragedy at Virginia Tech*. Her work has appeared in numerous publications and anthologies. She is working on a series of oil paintings depicting the Middle Passage.

Additional biographical information is available at **www.lucindaroy.com**